The Story of

David & [illegible]h

As told by

Pastor Chuck Smith

WITH ILLUSTRATIONS BY JOHN SHAFFER

The Word For Today, P.O. Box 8000, Costa Mesa, CA 92628 • Web Site: www.twft.com • E-mail: info@twft.com

The Story of David & Goliath
By Chuck Smith
With illustrations by John Shaffer

Published by The Word For Today
P.O. Box 8000, Costa Mesa, CA 92628
Web site: http://www.twft.com
(800) 272-WORD (9673)

ISBN: 978-1-59751-102-5

Scriptural quotations are based on the King James Version of the Bible unless otherwise specified. Translational emendations, amplifications and paraphrases are by the author.

Printed in the United States of America.

I WOULD LIKE to tell you a story about a boy named David.

David had many older brothers. His brothers were big and strong, and tough enough to fight in a battle.

When his
older brothers
were away, David
had to stay at home
and take care of
the sheep.

One day David's dad said, "David, your mother has made some cheese and bread for your brothers. Take it to them and find out how they are doing." So David headed off to the battle.

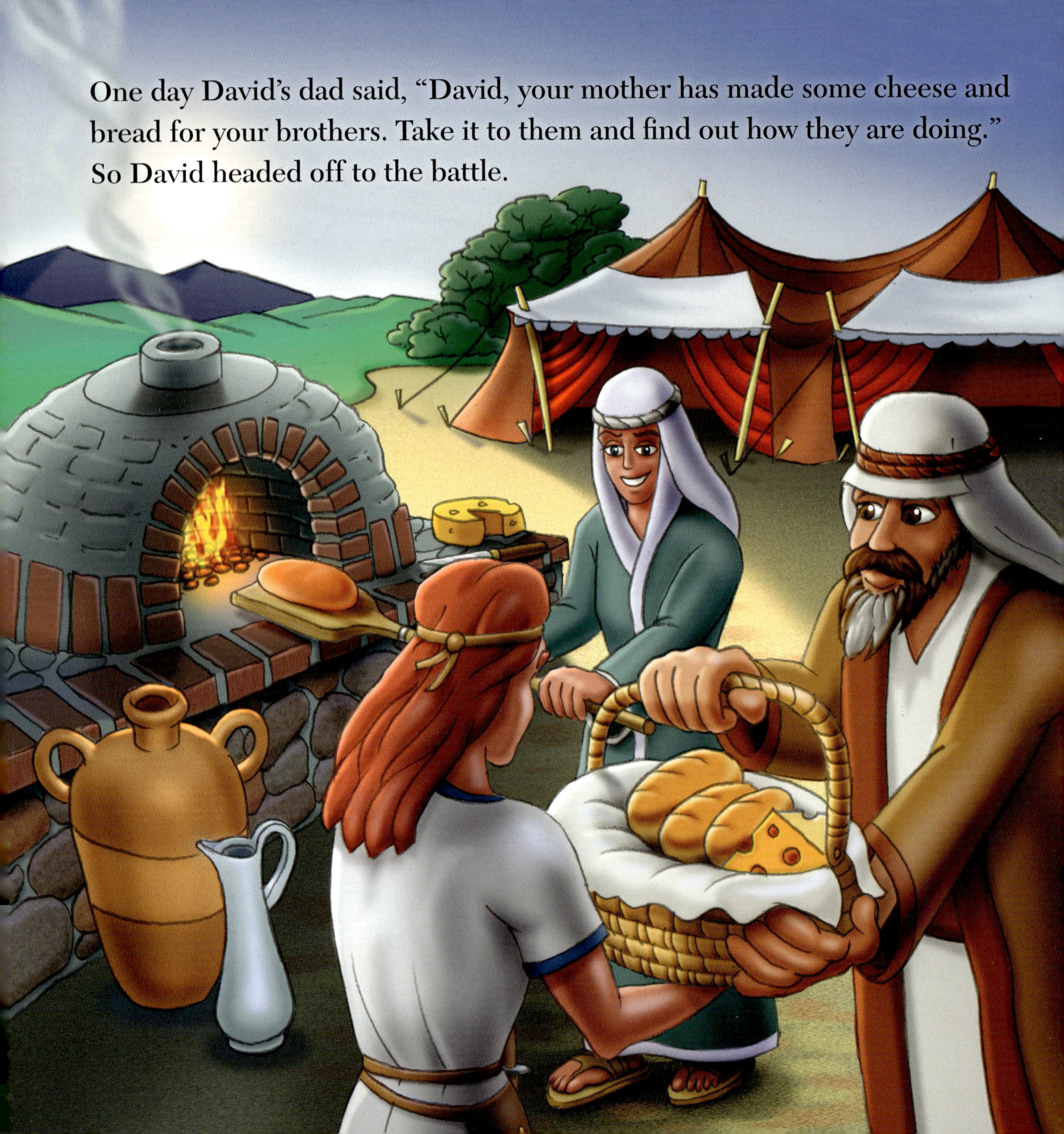

When David saw his brothers he said, “Mama made you some cheese and bread and Daddy wants to know how you are doing.”

Just then, David heard a loud, booming voice that thundered, “I am Goliath. Who will come and fight with me? If you win, then my men and I will serve you. But if I win, then you have to serve us.”

David looked around
and was surprised to see all of
the men of Israel trying to
hide—even his brothers!
David whispered,
"What is going on?"

Knowing that David was just the kind of boy that would never run from a fight, his brothers warned, “David, go home to Mom and Dad and don’t be a troublemaker!”

"What do you mean?"
David asked. "That man is
challenging you to a fight.
Why don't you go out and fight him?"

"He's too big.
He's over nine feet tall!
He's a giant!" his
brothers cried.

David said, "Look, if you don't want to fight him, then I will." David's brothers became angry. "David, get home right now!" they ordered. "We're going to tell Dad and you're going to be in big, big trouble."

"Wait a minute," David said. "We are the people who love God. This man is challenging God. Goliath cannot defeat God. He is not too big for God!"

In the meantime, the king of Israel was looking for a man to fight this giant, but everyone was too afraid.

David heard about the king's search and he volunteered. "I'll fight him!" Then someone ran and told the king. When the king heard about David, he commanded, "Bring me this man."

When King Saul saw David, he said, "You're just a little kid! Goliath is a man of war. You cannot fight that giant."

"Oh yes, I can,"
David replied.
The king looked down
at David and rubbing
his chin he asked,
"What makes you
think you can
fight Goliath?"

David answered the king. "One time when I was watching the sheep, a lion snatched a lamb and began to drag it off. I yanked the lion by the beard and I pulled the lamb right out of his mouth."

"Another time, a bear grabbed one of the sheep and I killed the bear. God helped me to slay the lion and the bear, so God will help me to slay this giant."

The king admired David's courage. "Okay, David. You can fight Goliath, but first, you must put on my armor." The king dressed David in a big, metal breastplate and gave him a large shield.

"Oh, this is too heavy," David said. "I cannot wear this. All I need is my sling."

David swung the sling above his head and let go of one of the straps. He let a stone fly past the king. The king smiled and said, “Go, David, and the Lord be with you.” So David went to fight the giant with just his sling.

On the way to the battle, David stopped by a little brook and he picked up five smooth, round stones to use with his sling.

With his five stones,
David climbed up the
hill to fight the big giant.
Goliath saw David and he
shouted, “Am I a dog that
you would send a child to
fight me? Go home, little boy,
or I’ll chop you up and
feed you to the birds!”

David was
not afraid.
He said to Goliath,
"You come against
me with a sword
and a spear, but
I come against you in
the name of God, whom you
have dishonored. I am going
to chop *you* up and feed
you to the birds!"

David reached into his pouch
and he pulled out a stone.
He placed it in his sling and
he swung it around ...

... and the stone flew toward the giant and hit him right in the middle of his forehead.

KABOOM!

Goliath fell flat on his face.

As Goliath lay on the ground, David grabbed the giant's sword and chopped off his head. Then David ran back to his brothers and said, "Look what God did!"

Everybody began to cheer—including David's brothers.

When Goliath's army, the Philistines, saw the giant fall down, they all began to run away. So the army of Israel, with David and his brothers, chased them.

Think about it. Because one little boy believed that God could do anything, a big, scary giant was defeated. David believed God was big enough, even to defeat giants. That day, God used David to win the battle for Israel.

Never think you are too little. God can use anyone who will just simply trust Him. It doesn't matter how big the giant is because the Bible says, "If God be for us, who can be against us?" (Romans 8:31).

It is important to know that God is for you. When God is for you, no one can defeat you. You will always win when you trust God.

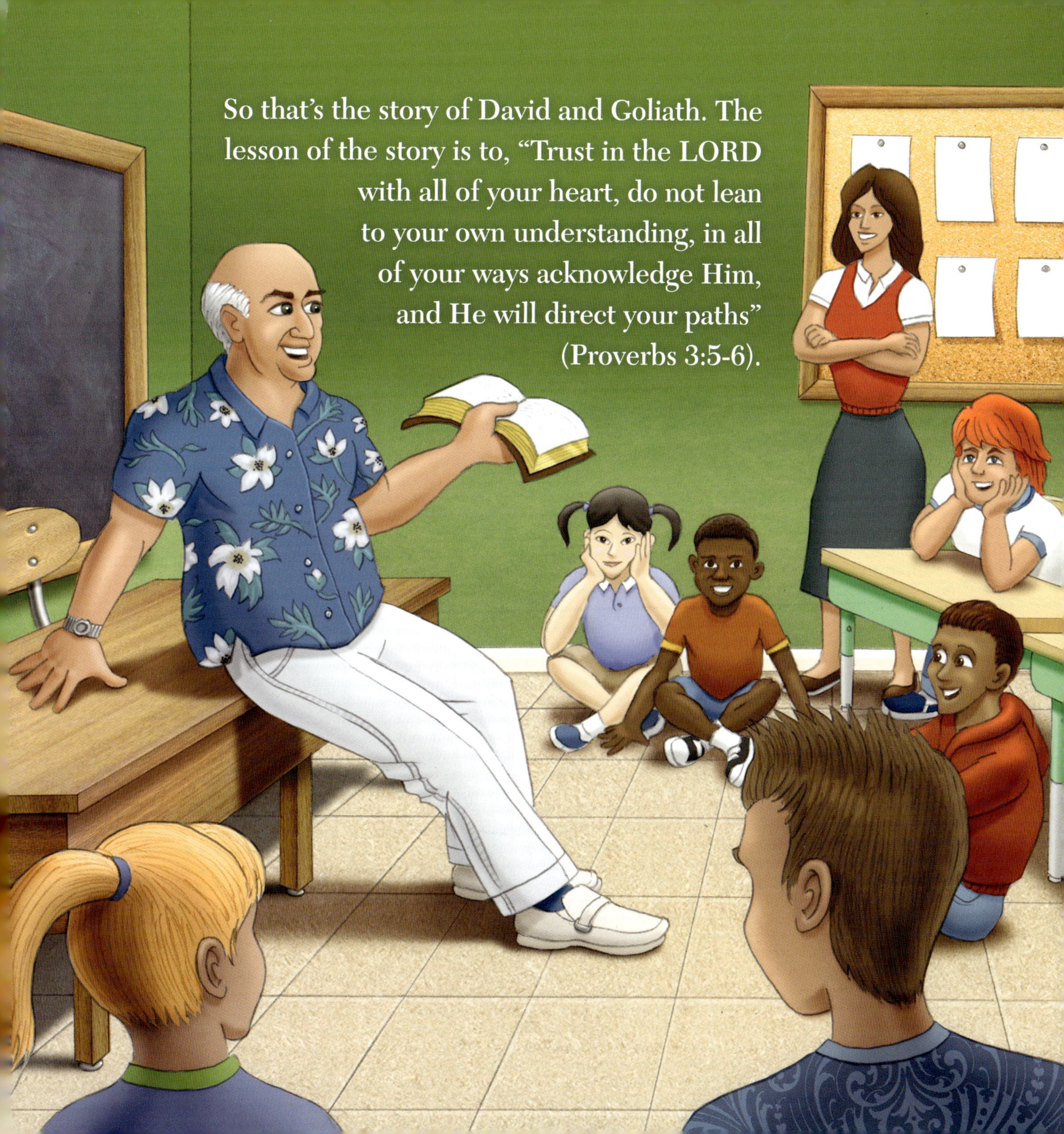

So that's the story of David and Goliath. The lesson of the story is to, "Trust in the LORD with all of your heart, do not lean to your own understanding, in all of your ways acknowledge Him, and He will direct your paths" (Proverbs 3:5-6).

The End